NEW LIFE

ANA BOŽIČEVIĆ

NEW LIFE

WAVE BOOKS

SEATTLE AND

NEW YORK

Published by Wave Books

www.wavepoetry.com

Copyright © 2023 by Ana Božičević

Wave Books titles are distributed to the trade by
Consortium Book Sales and Distribution
Phone: 800-283-3572 / SAN 631-760X

Library of Congress Cataloging-in-Publication Data
Names: Božičević, Ana, author.
Title: New life / Ana Božičević.
Description: First Edition. | Seattle : Wave Books, [2023]
Identifiers: LCCN 2022045040
ISBN 9781950268726 (hardcover)
ISBN 9781950268719 (paperback)
Subjects: LCGFT: Poetry.
Classification: LCC PS3602.O99 N49 2023
DDC 811/.6—dc23/eng/20220923
LC record available at https://lccn.loc.gov/2022045040

Designed by Crisis
Printed in the United States of America

9 8 7 6 5 4 3 2 1

First Edition

Wave Books 105

ZA TAMARU

Certainly the lordship of Love is good; seeing that it diverts the mind from all mean things.

Certainly the lordship of Love is evil; seeing that the more homage his servants pay to him, the more grievous and painful are the torments wherewith he torments them.

DANTE, *La Vita Nuova*, trans. Dante Gabriel Rossetti

> *Maybe she sleeps with eyes beyond all evil,*
> *Beyond things, illusions, beyond life,*
> *And her beauty sleeps with her, unseen;*
> *Maybe she lives and she will come after this dream.*
> *Maybe she sleeps with eyes beyond all evil.*

VLADISLAV PETKOVIĆ DIS

NEW LIFE

BIRTHDAY

If the sky is such a cliché
Why is it falling?

If the tree is such a cliché,
Why is it dying

If soul is such a cliché
Where is it hiding

If love is such a cliché
Why isn't there enough to go around.

For my part
I can't get enough of the sky.

For my part, I can't wait
For those leaves to come back.

For my party
I am inviting the clown Love

For my birthday I want a cake
Revealing the color of my soul.

NEW LIFE

I think about it
Every day
To just leave
And start life among some
Other people, in a little town
In the middle of America.
I would tell them
My name was . . . whatever,
Think of some random name
And say it.
I'd work in a diner
Put out the pie coffee
And burgers at the counter
The echo of
Great cities where
Everyone I ever loved
Everyone who ever hurt me
Anyone I ever hurtèd
Wouldn't reach.
Lost among fields
And mountains and highways
I wouldn't have anything

Much, unknown and safe
In witness protection
From crimes of the heart
Outside the merciless glare
Of my story
That blinds me
Bumps into me
Always spinning so I
See the back of her head
And her face all at once,
The one that tells me:
You failed to live me
Sang off tune
Like a shitty orchestra
And that's why
No one loves you enough
To stay!
Shut up Ana, I would say
The name's Linda.

I FEEL LIKE

An old vampire
In the middle of
War
Still made to feel like
A child
By the snow

WHO'S THAT

Eloquent
Silence of everyone I ever loved
This cloudy Friday evening
Spring but still cold
A smattering of new buds
Who's that
Swaddled in
The uneasy atmosphere
In silence
No chatter or pleasant surprise
The lusty rush of a weekend
With the beloved
Who's that
Sprouting now out of
The cottony silence
With silky whips
Still hanging from their little chops
Who is it straining
To pop out
Of the hardwood
Rings of time
Into the cool air

Like there's another cool world
On the other side of this one
Worth pushing
Through to or maybe
We're already there
Is that
Why we shake

I stood outside love's door
Afraid of what I'd find
A howling rainy void
A thousand clowns
The "It" from the phrase
"It's raining"—
The rain sounds
Like a bunch of eyelashes
Running around.
I tell tiny jokes to myself
In front of love's door—
I'm afraid I will find
No one there, an empty café—
Well that actually
Sounds nice.
I'd sit down and have
A cappuccino and one cigarette
And read those ancient
Newspapers back to back.
I stand outside love's door
Praying for
A soft landscape

To walk into,
Worn marble staircase
Some kind words, that's all.
Once I held love as a thing
And then it came
Alive in my hands, it
Bit, flowed like water . . .

SOFT POEM

I came
I slept
I came
I looked up
The sky was the blue
Of a baby-powder bottle
From a country
That no longer
Exists
The softest breeze
Touched the
Honeysuckle perimeter
I was feeling a
Little nice
Current in my body
Nikola are you with me
Gods of thunder
Ancestors
If I called out to you
Would you answer
In this land

WATERFALL

Everything in my room is so
Detailed you'd almost think
It was real
And it's getting harder
To play along with reality
I look long times
Out the window
Pretend
The room is a train car
For traveling through time
It's kind of true, it's how
The thing's designed
Or appears
And I have a secret weapon
I haven't spoken
A word aloud to a living person
All day
And I did this thing with time
It's hard to explain
Like sleeping
It makes you feel
Like everything's super funny

'Cause you can't get
Hurt when you say
Waterfall,
Water falling
Waterfall
Water falling
Waterfall
Water falling
Waterfall.

Instead of getting
Upset
That sometimes I wake up
Crying For No Reason,
I'm thinking
Maybe I am crying for
All the times I couldn't
And now I can
So it's all right
And then it stops.
All it needed was a little story.

EVERYDAY PEOPLE

Everyday people do remarkable things
They print new organs
Then insert them under the heart
Perform flawless gymnastics
Routines
They enter small metal pods
And glide through
The atmosphere
To the airless space beyond
They compose symphonies

Everyday people do impossible things
Bury their child on a warm
Spring day then make
A fresh pot of coffee
Feel pity and even forgiveness
For the person who wronged them
Stupidly, cruelly
Walk to the top of a mountain
And swim under ice
And still

Everyday people commit unspeakable crimes
They beat the bodies of elders
Who need their care
Tear children from parents
And put walls between them
Wipe out whole species
Level cities to nothing
Put poison in rivers
And on the trees they killed
Write beautiful poems . . .

ISLAND

For once in
My life
I got a bit of money
For writing a poem
About New York
I thought of all the things
I might do with my money
It would pay
For a trip home
To the as yet undiscovered
Blue island of the
Soul
I could throw a lavish party
And invite
All my friends
Pay all my bills
But no
Instead
I got bedbugs
I looked into the sheath
Where the money
Had been
The empty place
Laughed

Where is your island?
LOL. I smiled
I'm smiling
The room's quiet and the
Bugs are all
In heaven
For sure this day was one
For the memoirs
Tomorrow I will
Paint the room blue
And put the bed back in
It has to look good
For when the
Love of my life
Steps in through its door
And our whole world changes
But there's
Time
Tonight I
Sleep in the hammock
And tell my jokes to the
Cat
I'm drinking beer
This poem sucks
'Cause I'm so happy

5 THINGS AT 40

You are not crazy, it's the patriarchy
You're not a loser, it's the capitalism
You are not old, time's not really a thing
You're not alone, I'm here
You're made of stars, that's fucking cool

My heart is a drum majorette
Toy soldier with a broken arm
Falling into the sewer
What all could happen?
Riding the paper boat
Hope out to the estuary
Will we find the spring of youth
In the unassuming fountain
On the corner of St. Third
Or condense and fade
Like taxicab breath?
In whose sprawled out body
Did I make my home
Down whose blood am I
Rushing. The city is
A heart in the middle
Of which there's a garden.
Meet me there
Like the very first time
Before the Apple store
Made us feel naked
Let's find the grail

In an old sports trophy on
A dying villain's shelf
When I awake
From the coma
I want you to be there
Laughing in pajamas
I'll be the
One with the bouquet
From the underworld
And the toy heart
Sipping on a rain soda
Reading the rain newspaper

I was sitting in my rain study
Studious, soaking
When suddenly a letter flew in:
Alonsious, you must join us
At The Four Beers! At once
I sat on a beaker
And traveled there by picturing
I was a seagull feather
On a wave. That I was froth.

Well at least we
Got to meet
One another
In this place
Is what I imagine
Saying to my family
As we lock eyes
Clinging to the last
Plastic raft
On a giant wave
Whipped by
The nuclear blast—

An architect
Once built
A giant wave.
It stood suspended
Of an undefined
Indefatigable color
Above the town that
Would have stood
In its shadow,

Had it a shadow.
The wave seemed to utter,
Or did she?

Maybe it's a giant wave,
Maybe it's your own
Heart looming.
Where was I going
With this? I am going
To where the stream
Is always going,
Drawn along and
Pinned to the earth
By a Power
An enchantment
Rolling

With the purpose
Of Just Because.
Maybe I should
Get off the wave
Get out from under
The metaphor of the
Wave

Fly over the ocean
And go see
My father—
Is that all it takes?
Fly over the ocean

That sounds
Really hard and far.
I grew up in a little town
In the shadows
Of giant waves and now
I live in the city
Where I make small
Waves out of stone,
Everything here
Is made of stone
Even the cats—
That's my story.

When I get out of here
I'll see everything from above
like dream⁄me
instead of this ugly uneven wall
where a laterna magica
projects war twenty⁄four seven
and images of great feasts
from the courts we're not received
But even in heaven I'd probably
get offered a job in the lobby
and every now & then
they'd play your song
covered by the heavenly choir
to cover up the
constant wingbeats . . .

People are talking about the hum
or buzz of panic & war
preventing their daily functioning
and I keep thinking about
singing to the low C# drone
tonal vibration of the earth

once in a performance for hours
how shattering it was
just to walk around that stone chamber
trying to keep to the words
of the story expressed as canon
tapestry, orrery
like we were holding the earth up
& when the gala was over
we ate by ourselves in the dark

THE FUTURE

If somebody from the future
Tried to talk to me in the street
I wouldn't even know
'Cause I was listening to music

Our downstairs neighbor
Watered the
Concrete backyard
Twice a day religiously
To keep the dust
From his basement
Apartment until
The bare slab grew
Moss & lichen
Its own ecosystem
Water of life
We laughed at him but
One morning I went out
To the balcony hung
Over the backyard
To have a smoke—
Are you picturing
All this? It was
That time of month,
& I became
Light-headed
Bleeding through the white

Nightgown, I fell
& passed out for
A few moments
Woke with blood
Pooling
Around my head
& crotch—
But anyway, it was
Neighbor who found me and
Cared while I
Writhed in cramps
On his green love seat
Until the ambulance came
The ER was actually
Just a few blocks
Away and
When it was all done
I walked back the
Few streets over
Still in my long white bloody
Nightgown
& waist-long dark
Goth hair
A fresh stitch by my eye

Making a cross over
An old scar
Teen Madeline Usher
Or so I fancied
Walking through
Yards of dusty Zagreb roses
I wanted to control
The stream of time
Keep open the portal
To the parallel world
Where I was cared for
Something I somehow
Knew I deserved
I took on faith
As the first planes
Flew overhead

DEPRESSION

Is it programmatic
Or morally basic to say
There's a fucked-up glow
Inside me my friends
Don't really seem
To understand

Don't they see her.
Commercials
Show a somber
Dog or a cloud
Following you around
But she's a poet

An energy, she looks
Like me and you
Like our daughter
A future I couldn't
Pull off
Giggling on a swing

She looks like my
Mentor, my mother

Everyone I ever failed
Come to forgive me
For what I wish
They could help me

With. What soothes her
Is to go around the dead,
To bend my body
Tell me I'll never
Love again,
To leave me

Suddenly good and free
Then come
Back like the bad
Results from the polls
Like the first hard
Rain of the fall

And yeah, she can be
Kind of beautiful
In the mirror
And I love to be in her
Body when I'm
Lucid dreaming

I know why she wants to
Break through
To this side,
She brings with her
Galactic winds
And sometimes

I just want to ask her,
What is it? What is
So sad? And can the living
Help rather than be
Haunted?
How can I help.

Am I missing something,
The most important
Thing
Some
Key to healing,
Maybe her name . . .

.

If wishes were horses I would have no horse.
I opened my pussy and a crow flew in.
My heart is a dog sleeping
On our love's grave.
Yeah I've been keeping my
Heart open for you like an elevator
With my bare hands, and now
It's closing as fast as
The escape hatch
In the sci-fi movie. At the speed
Of a casket lid. The dog got up
Went to run along the sand.
In the distance, a rainbow.
Do I hear running water or horses running?

NULIFE

Dreamed of a new product
Called Nulife
Kind of like Ubik but not so volatile
Where you could just spray
Over your griefs, just spray joy
Over them, yay . . .
Picking up your life after a period
Of depression or reflection
Like a child
Handling vague beige triangles
Forever
Angels, bugs, distant lovers
Hungry for me to say it again
But I will never again
Say You again
Says my poor heart
The camera obscura wielded
By the soul, drunk again
And body tagging along
Asking shadow
Are you my friend
Asking the moon

Why won't you talk to me
But when the moon
Asks me out
I'm too shy to speak

NAOMI POEM

I dreamed of us falling asleep
In a garden holding hands
And our friends took a picture
And said They fell asleep
Like this

I PUT

bare feet in the fog
washed the sheets in ink
my heart in the fire
for you
I don't think I was ever
really a woman before
whoever found who
just an old high-top
abandoned at midnight
on the steps of your castle
When you like
a thing of mine
it's like being touched by a ghost
in a dream
of whoever's haunting who
Since you came
on my heart
I can't do anything
Wherever I go I
keep hearing this violin
that's how I know it's serious
I see your face

in clouds & in stucco
car alarms are bleating
your name
I stayed home
& danced with a potato
that looks like you

OPHANIM

I'm keeping quiet
And it's no use
When I look down
I'm saying your name
With all the lips
Your eyes look out
My tits
Your mouth IS
My heart
How did you climb
Inside of me
The little stick
Inside the violin
A second soul
Calling out for its skin
I've always known
There's a fire
A force
That midday beam
That pins everything
To the center
Of Earth

But like this?
Now I have 2 faces
Yours to mine
& a bunch of eyes
Everywhere that shine
Like the angel
In the icon
Whirlwind
Wheel on a wing
Praising who's
Making her sing

The clear thread of light
Across that tree
Is talking to me
And my soul
Overgrown and metastasized
From too little pruning
Or control
Rises to the front of my skin
Like a swimmer
To the rippling
Surface
Smells the tree
Sings to it
Ever since I was little
I let my soul have free reign
Inside me
Whoever tries to
Order it eventually goes away
Do you know
What it's like?
To have a wild garden
Inside you
Unassailably to

Watch it grow whole
Spires of thorn
To the sun
And meadows
Far as the eye can see
I watched my soul
Resurrect grandfather
Show me the stars
Even you
Fell in love with her
It couldn't have been me
And how I wish
Her mission ended there,
How I wish she'd stop
Before she wears me out
An old
Eastern European suit
Left in the dusty
Department store window
Faded from all the years of
Talking to the sun
Do you have any idea
The size of my soul
Baby

HEARTLAND

I have a sneaking suspicion
My heart is not mine
To give
It lives on a mountain
Buried in a field
Under miles of sod
I pity the fool, mostly myself,
Who'll
Have to dig it out.
I have a mind
To try taking someone there for
A change,
Pointing to the ground, saying
My heart is in here,
Do something.
Every time it faltered on you
Is 'cause it was so
Far, the connection distant—
Your heart beat next
To my empty chest while mine
Sent out signals

From an orchard
Across the ocean
Come find me it said
And other perfect things

PERSON

I want to be cool more than I want you to like me.
A disco ball wearing a crown of thorns.
Seaweed waving off the side of the underwater subway.
We started out as wood and morphed into silver in time.
It's 6 a.m. and I'm ready to go out and tell everyone else
    I'm a person.
And tell everyone I count as much as a penny.
I wished I could tell you I was more plausible than the
    night.
But you got stuck in the mirror labyrinth
And came out with a totally new name.
It's night-mornings like this I wish I could travel in time
Just to slap my own ass when I was born.

TREE

I imagine calling on witches
The whomen of my line
In front of me, a small tree grows
Getting bigger and bigger
Now it's the size of a mountain
I have to climb the tree
No one knows what I saw
On top of that tree

FREEFALL

The way u speak to me
Is it how you talk to your heart
In the end when everyone else is asleep
The fire out the water drawn
In lust
In the shower
Secret marginalia on dream rags
The way you talk to me
Would you talk to your own sun
That way
The one who lives in your heart
And looks at you through
My eyes
Keeps saying rise
And you try
After midnight, on the dark web
Looking for that most
Precious substance
I keep leaking
Like your heart
The car
Who was once a horse

Running
And running
In the shadow of the tall towers
With the first snow
Coming down

THE WIND

You smell like a
Cello to me
What I always
Wanted to play
You look like
A tree
With the light
Left on
I'm not sure
Where you came
From and what
Makes you afraid
But I know
It's not me
And you're not
From the past
I think you're
From some stream
Of time
That only
Just begins
Like a hiccup

I don't want
To end
Yawn passed on
In secret
The wind
Teasing the
Seafoam
Do you think
There's
Just one wind?

TREES SEE

Can cats tell the difference between a real and electric fire
Does cold air blow in or warm air flow out
Do you have dreams where you fly out a window.
The phone is like the windowpane slightly wearing your
    face
Your heart's a wet fire. That means you lack air
Your dream is the piece of toast you left in the toaster this
    morning

Did you ever see your reflection on top of a picture of you?
Did your shadow ever cross the projector.
The phone is like a painting I can bring you up in
From outside, I see your face inside a frame
When I am standing looking out my window
From outside, the tree sees my face in the frame
Behind me my favorite shadow hangs.

LONG LINES

Looked around your life &
Found no place to sit
So I've just been standing
This whole time
And every time I look in
Like that I see
A different color room
Full of beautiful strangers
Who care less
Ever since those childhood
Queues for TP & brown bread
I leave when I see
Long lines
With what relief
I breathe the smog
Tuck into an empty alley
Holding suddenly
Giant church steps
I sit here & smoke

REQUIEM FOR GEORGE MICHAEL'S HOLOGRAM

I snapped to
In the middle of the dream party
When at the same time
Across the room
You did the same
We looked up
And locked eyes
We were the only ones
Aware this side of sleep
In a city full of dreamers
Living their best and worst
Lives, we
Were wide awake
And in a fantastic mood
"What are the odds" I
Looked down and saw
Four perfect red leaves
In an almost random
Pattern on the raw concrete
And laughed
I had made this world

In all its detail and so
It was real
"This is real," I said
"Let's get out of here"
Outside in the street we went
To try flying
We held hands and rose
And flew all over
The little city mists clung
To high balconies
The last pine tree
Shone by a
Billionaire's roof pool and we flew
Up into the clouds
Holding each other's
Elbows like ballroom dancing
"It's real!" we kept saying
And laughing
It's a dream but it's
Real
This is real. Then I woke up
This time for real?
The only one still
Dreaming in the city of

The living
I am old here and time
Goes by in weird eddies
And loops
They inject my system
With viruses
Fatigue, trauma, anxiety
And you're floating away from me
A good song
From a passing car
Everyone's always going
Away here
Forgetting their dreams
Redeployed
By desire aka economy
Except yours truly
Condemned to level one
By my failure to
Dance along with the code
Believe in the city
The rain
That I should just
Let it all play out
But it's not real

I know by how they keep playing
Back the song from
The dream
To remind me of all
I've lost, just to
Drive it home
I'm never gonna dance again

ARS POETICA

Late at night
When I was relaxed enough
To see what the aliens were doing
I saw a machine
Drop scrolls of light
Into my water
It's where all the poems come from

It's 3:26 a.m.
In New York
Listening to "Under the Gun"
By The Sisters of Mercy
Maybe
If I was a thick-skinned binch
Who loved money
America would love me
But it won't
And I'm not
It's hard to feel like a gun
Is pointed at
Literally everything
Life and love especially
I won't be there
In the condo with you
To listen to the last broadcast
From planet Earth
Mainlining drugs
In North America or
Western Europe
When money

Runs it all into the ground
I won't make a sound
I'll be in the forest
Up the mountain from
My dead
Collecting pine nuts
For the long ride
Home to the sun
Well really most likely
I'll be on the subway
Listening to
Some song

SIGH

You have the effect
On me
Like finding out Kurt Cobain died
Alive you are
A famous suicide
And in a world
So full of unsexy drear
At least yours is hot
But I've loved other
Cool people like you
And in the end it's always sad
And I feel so cold
At the crossroads
In the crown of a great tree
In the light rain.
I wish I could go back to my sea
And forget this
Country and your band.

TRASH MOON

All my life I had stage fright
O wonder terror of being called to the front
To recite in a dialect, sing, answer questions on
    alchemical elements
Once in school during wartime I was so drunk
I just wrote H_2O on the blackboard and sat down on
    the ground
And I so wanted to be part of a chorus
I injected vitamins
Still when I got to the tryouts
I couldn't make a sound
Mom ran after me, crying all the way home
But the worst of all
Was once playing with friends and you were there
When I realized
No matter how well I played and sang
It wouldn't change a thing
So I couldn't sing
When you left I sat on the curb
Smoked one
Then reached into my throat and
Pulled out the moon
Threw it into the trash and walked away

more than ever
time feels like a river
bringing you closer
if I can only make it upstream
ten years or
ten hours
I get to see tes yeux
so I sail
along the banks of morning
thronging with ghosts
into the eye of noon
hope you'll be waiting
on the shore of evening
but it's night
I'm out in the open
still rowing

I WOULD LOVE TO

I would love to be
Old and
Beloved
Freely like water
A joyous elder
High up where I see
The start and
The end
Of the silver
Mountain

I'd love to be
Your daughter
Someone for whom
You would do
Any thing in any
Weather
A baby braid
On the rafter
Snow flower
Coming back

It's okay
To grow out
Of the snow
For a season
Lovers rush
Through life like
Mountain fires
I'd love to just call you
Friend and
Hang forever

EVIL TWIN

The time I snapped at mom for ugly-crying at *Love Actually*.

When I stand on the subway full of other men and feel I am surrounded by stronger enemies.

The time I developed a whole dialectic around why you suck for not loving me.

When I postponed replying to an email until the person died.

When I didn't visit my grandparents and then they died.

I won't tell you I love you and we will die.

Or I tell you and you don't care and then we die.

I didn't apply to my dream job.

I didn't finish the novel or the album.

I let the one I love leave forever and then I didn't even
    love them anymore.

I didn't care if I lived or died. I cried all the time.

I thought people were staring at me 'cause there was
    something wrong with me but really

It's because I'm so tall and handsome.

THE GIFT

I strayed from
The road to town
Walking to my wedding.
I became lost
In the woods. Wandered
Through untold
Old acres of deep-
Rooted trees trying to
Find a way out for years
While my beloved
Believed the lies
They told about me
Believed our last
Fight
Frowned at
My memory and let
It fade. What if
While she was forgetting
I wandered on
My white dress
Now gray
Blond hair turning gray

My lung blue
And white from the sun.
What if at last
I found a way out of
The woods and walked
Into town
Up to her house and
She looked out at
Me. What if I looked
So much now
Like my grandma, whom she
Once loved. "Ms. B?"
She says, hesitantly.
I smile and hold out a
Small mushroom

SATURDAY

A mighty opponent
Picked me off—
A feather—

And I knew
God was fake
When you left

But even as a
Brokenhearted
Zombie I get

How special it is
That I am alive
With my brother

Eating ice cream.

&

Who do I write to
If you're long gone.
When people say,
It's between myself
And God
What if the God part is off?
Someone turn God
Back on!
The kind that
Makes me feel like
It's the same
If I write to you or Them
Or to an old
Long piece of wood that
Lay by the stable—
I know it's
Not supposed
To be permanent,
None of it and no one, so
Why did They
Make it so precious
Then. Are people

Destroying everything
Out of the need
To take
And keep everything?
Yes. For me,
I don't
Need much
But the comfort
Of another world
The parallel universe
Where somehow
It worked out
And birds are singing,
There is peace
When you & I
Are an ampersand away
God's in
The ampersand . . .
But no one says
Our names together
Anymore
We wholly ghosted
Each other
& it's been a long time

Since I talked to God—
They got too high
And thought
They were dying
Sent me a postcard
From heaven
Saying I hate the sun
And I miss
Lucifer
The middle manager
Turned crook
He picked a better animal
To hide in
The snake that
Still on some nights
Forms an ampersand
& thinks of love.

GOD IS DEPRESSED

God was let go
God is on unemployment
God sits around in sweats
And binge-watches
"Are you still watching?"
I'm always watching
From the beginning
Of time
And I still see
You my child
I'm just too depressed
To stop
The world I made

MOONWHATEVER

I've gotten so used
To being alone
But sometimes when you give me
A hug
I remember what it was like
And my glands burn in
That sour river of radness
Either way I
Stand like a tree
Getting hugged
And I think that's pretty funny.

MOONRING

While I sit here thinking
Of the apocalypse
Leaves are bouncing
Moonbeams against my window
Like heartstrings
Did they always know
This song?

After all the shows
I've watched and stories
I read
After what I saw my family
Survive will I stand and
Fight
Fight against what?

Tell me, moonbeams
Little fists
Smacking the window
Which way to turn and in
What language to say
What thing
And to whom.

I keep thinking
I don't deserve to be here.
Not in this body
This family
Not in this country or the other.
I keep thinking
I need to do something

And I do all the things
With the dread and joy
Of someone cursed hoping.
Eyes in my fingernails
Stare me in the eye
When I type
They are my honor

Every word a nail
Holding a promise to
A wall . . . will it be full
In the end of desperate notes
Crafted by moonbeams
In seasickness
Or totally empty?

This time of month
I leave myself a ring
On a beam of moon
That I can wear again
When I'm small enough again
To bear the weight
Of my name.

WIND 2

I used to look for
The titration of your name
In the shivering leaves
In twinkling stars
Wrinkling water
But now I don't.
The leaves move
Saying their own thing
Doing their old thing
The dance duet
Where the invisible one
Is the stronger
The leaves don't know you
You're like the wind.

He writes sad scores for TV shows
And at night he listens to the
DJ Silence
Spinning rooftops
Or mountains
The grain silos of Massachusetts
Rising like
Sad dicks
In the aging summer
The fireflies
Are dying
I want to move to Buffalo
And live forever

UNTITLED

You were a teenage goth
In wartime
Spent years in the
Emotional labor workshop
To love is to lose everything
First to joy
Then to pain
Until after
The brief exit interview with
The priest
They're all texting at
Your funeral

Until you pass
Through death
And get to that other place
And I don't mean
Heaven
The intake room
Decompression chamber
For turning to stars
Where bones are

Milled into fire
And you are finally seen
The way you see

The world from inside
Your current body
And understood
And pitied and loved, carried
Away on complex
Vast cosmic trajectories
Down rings ringing with
Ultraviolet vibes
That only a young energy unicorn
Could hear
Your final loss
Will be amazing

On my machine
I saw wondrous things
A building pointy like a
Stiletto
A glacier folding
And floating past a village
Your whole new
Life
And the life
I can project outward
Like the sun
Throwing flares
To preclude
Implosion within
On my machine

I've seen wondrous things but
Never like
When you come
Into a room and light
Shines through
Radioactive
Like there was

Something to it all
In the end
And it was gonna be okay
On a show I watch I saw
A pirate say
"I'm ruined over you"
And that's how I feel

A heart X-ray
No, heart xerox
Revealed
A peeling room in a crypt
A awful literary
Fate
Of poverty and exile
"Authenticity"
And a whole other pile of
Demons
That I can't shake
To be like you
Like air

Like the drums
Of a drummed up
Kingdom.

Punked and
Drunk on the breath
Of the second world
I made
I sleep and wait
To be delivered
From my pains of want
By what
I have no idea

And in a dream
I saw the perfect
Village
And everyone I loved
So young
And even the
Animals I loved
All resurrected
In this babely haven
Under the fir trees
Tossing

A silver ball back and forth
And calling

To me
Ana
To forget my misery
And come among
My family and
Know
What love is again
And endless time

A A
   N
But then, remember
How you
Said it to me
The N in my name
Dark as wood
A tree trunk
From which grow

Two vowels of light
It's a crown of
Light.
And I forsake
My family and friends

And follow
You through the woods
And I sit in peeling rooms

Waiting for that light
To roll on through
Like ball lightning
Eerie and
Swampy now
Coloring evening
In cemetery pink

Making every thing
And everyone I love
Be crinkled
Dead
Flowers with its flash
It couldn't

Possibly be love
This awful
Light, could it?
So what are you
Then?

What do you mean
By shedding
Yourself onto life
Until it's the color

Of death, graying and
Crinkled flowers?
If you're not love

Then you're
Not my light,

I'll be the light.

Nikola Tesla fell in love
With a pigeon
Nikola Tesla died
In a hotel room
In New York City
Destitute and abandoned
Like some Keats
Of science
And now
A few miles from where
Nikola Tesla was born
My little brother
Writes sci-fi
Water's getting harder
And family bones
Dry underground
While a lonely lightbulb
Illuminates the
Checkered tablecloth
I eat bread and cry

ODE TO THE ☀

I follow the others
Across the crosswalk
Face to the sunlight
Sun
This is where we
Part ways
It might be the last time
I see you today
Descending into
The underground where I am
Spelled to spend
How much of my life
Thundering on trains
Deep in dreams
Locked forever in a neon box
Illuminated by a digital
Screen
High up in the air
In the forest of stories
Where a stray
Ray of sunlight
Sometimes seeks me out

Like being
Touched by a thought
Bright star
Do I worship you when
I like to burn things
And will the
Burning
Bring me back to you again
I set my life on fire
Its warmth
Feels like love on my face

When you had a wet dream
the fairies stole your DNA
and made a clone
of you, only a mermaid
sometimes you catch her
thoughts inside of you
like little toes
anemones
just admit it you
love that word
she sees a misty
green cave at the
bottom of the great drop-off
you see her enter an
establishment in an
algae trench coat
she's there to rescue
your soul from the
unscrupulous barkeep
and she outdrinks him
and leaves at dawn
with your soul on a little

golden leash
by now New York City
is mostly underwater but
when she surfaces
from the long dark tunnel
and sees the sign
that used to say
NOSTRAND AVENUE
she knows she'll find you
still in the same place
dreaming while your bed
slowly bobs down the
city waters
gently she places
your soul inside
your rib cage
and swims away
as the flood recedes
or maybe she keeps
the soul for herself
'cause feelings are cool

ODE TO A ☁

another summer in New York
something always keeps me,
sometimes sadness sometimes love
well mostly love
by different names
like fear
then some salt breeze talks
through the window
that old line
"sky the color of your eyelids"
or the future
hiding the fun
behind a cloud of clouds
is the last thought in my mind
that cloud from a TV show
things come and go
I just said that
'cause it rhymed and I
still believe in beauty

There we were
Two astronauts
Hanging out in front of the huge blue orb
Encased each
In our own life-support system
Chatting about the polls
Love & life on Earth
The only thing between us
A trembling
Silver chord . . .
How long has it been
And in that time
Have we learned
Anything about the planet below us
Developed an out-
Of-our-caskets scenario
Ground control
Emphasizes the importance of the mission
But hanging here
It feels like
Your brown eyes are
All I know of Earth

And life support
And on some turns
When we talk about space & time
& the silver line between us
Shimmers
It almost seems
The vacuum grows air
In the space between us
Like we made it safe
And don't you wonder what would happen
If we took off our helmets
Just once to kiss
Would we explode or freeze
Like a solar Rodin
Cautionary tale
Star at the end
Or evolve into a new thing
That needs something else to breathe

SOMETIMES

Sometimes I ride in on my horse
Singing
Like a shepherdess
To another shepherdess
At the edge of the woods
To avoid loneliness
Since you visited me
A couple of times
Strange one
I haven't known peace
Dreaming of
Eerie palaces
Waterfalls at night
I lived in the development
Over your grove
And you came out
Funny little you
And touched my heart's lips
You showed me rabbits
Bluebells in a sudden clearing
We flew up and saw
The tops of trees

Passing under us
In waves
Between the crowns and clouds
We made a promise
Never to make promises
But I made one anyway
Put a double rainbow
Over the ruined castle
With a touch of your finger
You set it on fire
The rainbow is burning

NAOMI POEM 2

While you dream
I synchronize
My breathing to yours
It's like we are rowing together

SUPERSTAR

People
Have many names
For a
Woman who fails
To see the features of God
In a single face
But what if I were to say
The thing I chased
Never stayed in just one body
What if I told you
I was following a spirit

Tumbling in the fog
See you appear
And are you here to stay
This time
Or move on, shadow
On your silver lining
With that collar up
Against the mind
Blowing from your eyes
Knocking me down

By the time I got up
You were gone

I know the
Crime is in trying but
Saw you're playing in heaven
So I'm going
Across islands
Of time
To sit at that bar with a star
An actual star.
Hear your words divine
Lie to everyone later
They're mine

TRIALOGUE

Some days my body fits weird like a
a stiff glove over an anemone . . .

Some days it feels like my body is an organ America
    keeps rejecting. Thinking of someone else while
    making love to me.

Someone surely has a rag doll of my body strapped to
    the hood of their dirt truck.

And the gods that come in and out of me like

Fish in and out of the tiny old
Chest at the bottom of the aquarium . . .

Marked by gods
Jealous, they never leave me

They send out a cicada to destroy me

GLITTER

Now you talk to me flame
When all is said & done
When everyone's gone
Chance of love & fame
& change
Now you come to me flame
When no one will listen
When I'm tired, hanging by a nail
With my hand out to catch the alpine flower
I spotted in the ravine at sunset
When all's good as done
Dauphine
You come and say my name

X X X

I stepped out of the shower
Steaming like a glazed donut
I was getting ready for work
I know they want us to hate this part
But I don't. I alter my mind a bit
And put on a really slow song
I plan to be late
Standing forever in the
Sunshine at the crosswalk
Thinking about you
And how it was kind of nice
Just sitting there next to you
Tryna glimpse your fingers
From the side of my eye
Figure out how they'd feel inside
Suddenly like the light
Fills the piazza

ENDLESS HEART

My heart is a vinyl stuck on repeat
I pulled my heart up off the floor
Heavy meat curtain
And went to bed
To touch along to a poem
This is sad
The yellow bird dreams
Land and depart
You've gone off
And made many movies but
I'm still in this little old town stuck on you
At night when you sleep inside
Your swan do you think of me
Ever
You make me wanna
Buy a computer and write really long lines

My heart is a pink knife
I keep by my bed
My meow
My heart's grown a beard wrapped around
Its bone throne in the mountain

Somewhere by a sea
You pass through fogs
The most intense colors bloom inside
The funniest jokes on repeat
I flew here to see you
We talk against seagulls like
Bright commas on
Night mode
And I don't even care
How I end a poem
How I end a poem

SAD WATER

Fell asleep
Holding my phone
Like a weird little
Metal bird
Woke up to rain
In the window,
Wherever I go
It will rain there too
At least water
Can be trusted
Wish I trusted you
The way I
Trust metal
I was a new phone in
Your hand, a bird
In your palm,
Et cetera.
I had
This idea that
Rain is nature's TV
Maybe it's the water inside
Me that's sad

That's how you get hanged
Because the inspector was held up
By street works on the way to
Stop your execution
Because the one you love
Quietly, coldly let life
Fritter away & burn like a french fry
In the summer
Well I'm here to say
To hell with all that & if you
Thought you owned surrender
And could force it on me
You have another world coming

I'm
What's left after the poem has been written
The excess
Cream, dew, froth
That makes up my flesh
Yes implacable
Carried by the wind that deafens anyone
In its path of pure matter
Spinning to an untimely beginning
As something else
Pity me
No longer a woman
Pity me
No longer a body to be cherished
But some extra cloth
Cut up
For shrouds or flags for her barricades

LAST STAR

I counted my loves
Is it true I'm still in life?
I counted my lives
If it's true I'm in love then
I'm on my ninth. Gulp.
All the boys I loved
Home with their wine & wives
All the girls are in loves
The wolves are in the wood
I sit here with the poplars
Trying to feel like
I am matter
Here in my last life
Wearing a thin, perfect
Piece of paper . . .
In how many hearts
Has this love burned
Why have I been passing it on
What did I want
To give them, and what
Get back
Not faith & touch?

No sure return and
It does, the freedom I give
Has a price
Women like me
Have a name
Look it up in the big book
The part about breasts
& kingdoms
So what did I want?
I asked the poplars.
To live, to live, to live . . .
And for once
No matter what I did
To feel like I guided
Your movements like seasons
A star in your heart
You just can't put out

THE PHILOSOPHERS

Every place I arrive to
I wonder
If I am okay with this being
My last place
And if I am okay leaving
Maybe never coming
Back
But that's so heavy
Wouldn't it be nice
To just come and go
Without a thought
To how long and who
Without the need to know?
I have to know.
For days I wouldn't say
A word, my <3
Held its breath
Wanting to know
What no one knows.
That's why I like
Hanging out with you,
Make me forget

Entirely such questions
Leave them to the
Philosophers—us two
When, left alone,
We don long beards
And stare long nights
Into the skull and candle
Like the bards
And maidens of old
Through plagues and wars . . .
And we're still
Kind of young.

U S

whatever happens
I just have to remember
how you feel
when I put my hands
to your chest
your soul a lightbulb
flashing just under your skin
what happens happens
this did
the membranes were thin
enough to let us eat light

BRUNO'S ELEGY

What to make of
This mew afterlife
Alone in a rented room
Whose dirty windows
Let the sun in like
A paused prayer
Three green apples
On my table
Three bottles of
Bubbly water
And three personas
Daytime nighttime
And hybrid
Bleeding into one
Dialectical
Montage from a Raymond
Chandler picture
Mother, it is the oneliness
You feared for me,
But I don't even
Have feelings
Like that anymore

Just observe the angels
Riding dust motes
Down a sunbeam
In an endless
Circle of returns
To make Start possible
Hit Return—
Or so my avatar said
To a beauteous girltaur
In the streets of my mind
Bruno Schulz and I
Pass by the sculpture of
A giant tote
The hourglass still hangs
Above the old sanatorium

HAPPY ENDING

I saw a movie
Called *james white*
In which a son

Tells his dying mother
(there's no dad in the picture)
About the perfect life

She never had
He tells her they're living
In paris

& she's
Surrounded by friends & fam
A loving boyfriend

And is beautiful & treasured
In her own right
But in reality

She's retching & he's
Holding her on the bathroom floor
And that's love

That's what i wanted
To do for u
To paris

We'd go and eat the moussiest cheese
And to tokyo and sample
Mushrooms off a plate

Dressed as the forest floor
And i'd look
Fabulous

And u'd look however
U wanted to look
Because there's no part

Of u that's not
Ideal to me
From when u were born by the sea—

But we can't
Because
The world

& we're broke and fighting
& still have (i feel)
Too much

Now i feel
We need to go somewhere
Else

A field of clouds
Then a beach—
The one where u are married

To some new love of ur life
And i attend
And even sing a song—

Even though i might not
See into loving
Anyone beside u

Anyone after u
And even if
I'm as happy as

Gatsby when i see
That green light
On the messenger light up

From across
The dark dark
Water—

I will be at ur deathbed
If u want me there
And at ur funeral

I won't be shy about
My love
And i'll see u

When we're particles
Or ghosts
Baby

And that's love
That's what i want
To do for u

Would u do the same
Can u even
Maybe u just

Can't even
And not even knowing
Whether u do

Well that's love too
Its own meaning
It's what i've been meaning

To talk to u about
Now let's talk about something else—
Like what

I would like
In an ideal
World

I'd like
Fight and fuck
Rather than fight

And fall apart
I'd like to pick u up
At an ancient island airport

So happy u r there
And that that's life
I would like

To know that when
Alien teens
Find these notes

We write about
Each other
At some distant time

When all that's left
Of u and me
Is dew—

They will say
Wow
Do u see how in love

They used to be
It wasn't just
Literature

The carnival
Of selves
It was real love

That force that rolls
Thru everything
& powers the stars

& they'll speed away
But life is not
A godard movie

Not an early one anyway
It's more like
Jlg/jlg

In which
Over footage of green fields
Opening

With the trust i recognize
He says *i said*
I love

That is the promise
By which he means
As long

As i love
I know
That love exists in the world

ACKNOWLEDGMENTS

Poems in this book have appeared in *Bedfellows Magazine*, *The Believer*, *Big Lucks*, *blush* (*Spring City*, 2021), *Brooklyn Rail*, *can we have our ball back?*, *The Equalizer*, *Foundry*, *Green Mountains Review*, *Iterant*, *Jewish Currents*, *New York Tyrant*, *Poetry Daily*, *PoetryNow* at the Poetry Foundation, *Pouch*, *Prelude*, and *Recluse* at The Poetry Project.

"I Stood Outside" is after John Wieners.

"Weak Signal High Quality" is for Weak Signal & BHQF.

"Nulife" is after Han Shan.

"Naomi Poem" and "Naomi Poem 2" are after Saint Geraud/ Bill Knott.

"Sigh" is after Zvonko Karanović.

"Nikola Tesla Fell in Love" is after Viktor Vida.

"Superstar" is for Diane di Prima and after "The Poetry Deal."